William Tecumseh Sherman

MILITARY LEADERS OF THE CIVIL WAR

Don McLeese

Rourke
Publishing LLC
Vero Beach, Florida 32964

www.rourkepublishing.com

PHOTO CREDITS: P 06 Department of the Interior
P13 Mahn Center for Archives and Special Collections/Ohio University Libraries, all other images from the Library of Congress

Title page: Sherman and Union officers at the Battle of Chattanooga in 1863.

Editor: Frank Sloan

Cover and page design by Nicola Stratford

Library of Congress Cataloging-in-Publication Data

McLeese, Don.
  William Tecumseh Sherman / Don McLeese.
     p. cm. -- (Military leaders of the civil war)
  Includes index.
  ISBN 1-59515-478-7 (hardcover)
  1. Sherman, William T. (William Tecumseh), 1820-1891--Juvenile literature.
2. Generals--United States--Biography--Juvenile literature. 3. United
States. Army--Biography--Juvenile literature. 4. United
States--History--Civil War, 1861-1865--Campaigns--Juvenile literature. I.
Title.
  E467.1.S55M35 2006
  355'.0092--dc22

                              2005010982

Printed in the USA

Rourke Publishing
1-800-394-7055
www.rourkepublishing.com
sales@rourkepublishing.com
Post Office Box 3328, Vero Beach, FL 32964

Table of Contents

~

Sherman's March

~

Of all the Civil War **generals**, few were more famous or more feared than William **Tecumseh** Sherman. As a general of the **Union** army of the North, he led his **troops** on a march on the South in 1864. The South hated Sherman. When he and his **soldiers** marched through the South, they raided houses and set fire to buildings. They thought that ruining the homes and cities of the Southern people would make the South give up.

The North thought Sherman was a big hero. After the war was over, both the Democratic and Republican parties wanted him to run for president. He said no. Being remembered as a great general was enough for him.

Sherman became a hero to the North after the Civil War had ended.

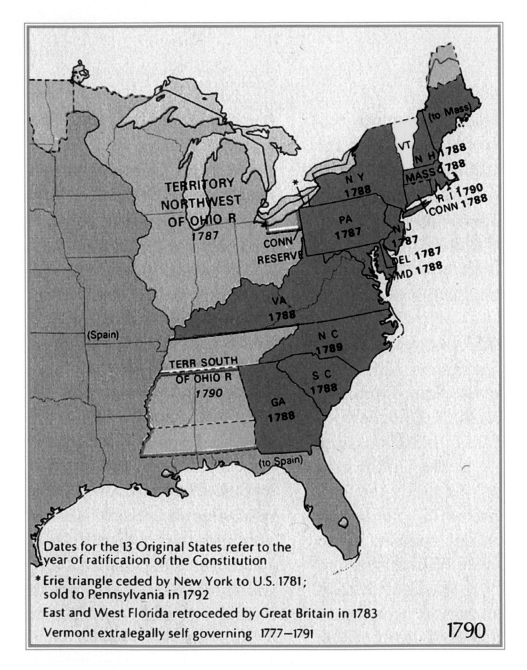

Dates for the 13 Original States refer to the
year of ratification of the Constitution

*Erie triangle ceded by New York to U.S. 1781;
sold to Pennsylvania in 1792

East and West Florida retroceded by Great Britain in 1783

Vermont extralegally self governing 1777–1791

1790

*Ohio became a state in 1803. Before then,
it was part of the Northwest Territory.*

Born in Ohio

~

Tecumseh Sherman was born on February 8, 1820. He was the sixth child of Charles and Mary Sherman. The family lived in Lancaster, Ohio. Sherman's father was a lawyer and a judge. In those days, when the country was not even 50 years old, Ohio was considered part of the "wild west," or the **frontier**.

"Cump"

~

Tecumseh's family usually called him "Cump," a nickname that stayed with him for the rest of his life. This was short for "Tecumseh." His parents had given him this name in honor of a great Native American warrior.

As a chief of the Shawnee tribe, Tecumseh was a leader who wanted peace but who would fight bravely if he needed to. Tecumseh Sherman would also work for peace and be willing to fight for it.

Tecumseh: This Shawnee chief tried to bring all the tribes of Native Americans together so they could keep their land. His name means "shooting star."

8

Sherman's namesake, the Native American chief Tecumseh

A photograph of the schoolhouse Sherman attended in Ohio

His Father's Death

~

When Cump was only nine years old, his father died. Cump now had ten brothers and sisters. His mother could not support such a big family on her own. She sent her children to live with different friends and relatives. Cump went to live with Thomas Ewing, a lawyer who had been a good friend of Cump's father.

The Ewings already had six children, but they gave Cump as much love as they gave any of their own. They also gave him a new first name: William.

The Ewings had a son, Phil, who was the same age as Cump. The two became best friends and did everything together. When he grew up, Cump married Phil's sister, Ellen.

Off to West Point

~

Becoming part of the Ewing family helped Cump become a **military** officer. When Cump was 16, he went to West Point in New York. He wanted to study to become a general.

Like a lot of boys his age, Sherman didn't always obey the rules. He got into some trouble at West Point. "I was not considered a good soldier," he said. But he was a very good student. When he graduated in 1840, he was sixth in his class!

Senators: Two senators are elected from each state. They go to the U.S. Congress in Washington, D.C., where they help make the laws of the nation.

12

As a senator, Thomas Ewing was able to get Sherman into the U.S. Military Academy at West Point.

Soldiers at a camp in Florida during the Second Seminole War

Fighting the Seminoles

~

The army sent William Sherman to Florida, where there were battles with a tribe of Native Americans called the **Seminoles**. The Seminoles wanted to stay on the land in Florida that had long been their home, but the United States wanted the tribe to move west. The two sides fought from 1835 to 1842.

William Sherman arrived toward the end of what was called the Second Seminole War. He was a member of the artillery, the group with cannons and other powerful firearms.

Seminoles: This tribe moved from what is now Alabama and Georgia into what is now Florida in the 1700s. The tribe's name means "runaways."

15

West to California

~

In 1846, the army sent Sherman to California when the Mexican War started. The land that is now California was then part of Mexico. William helped those Americans living there fight to become free of Mexico. The war ended in 1848, with the United States paying Mexico $15 million for more than half a million square miles of land in the west and southwest.

California: It didn't become a state until 1850, shortly after the end of the Mexican War.

American forces land at Vera Cruz, Mexico, during the Mexican War.

Sherman is shown in an undated photograph.

A Family Man

~

William continued to live in California after the war ended. But in 1850, he returned east to marry his childhood sweetheart, Ellen Ewing. The two of them would raise a big family: four boys and four girls. William and Ellen lived for a while in St. Louis, but in 1852 they returned to California. They lived in San Francisco.

William left the army in 1852. Now that he was married with children, he wanted a job where he could make more money and stay home with his family. He worked for a bank in San Francisco and then moved with his family to Kansas.

In 1860, a new college opened in Louisiana for young men who wanted to become soldiers. William became head of this school.

19

Louisiana Leaves the United States

~

While the Sherman family lived in Louisiana, there was trouble between the states of the North and those of the South. The Northern states wanted to make slavery illegal. They said it was wrong for a person to own another person.

The Southern states said they would leave the United States and become their own country if it became illegal to own **slaves**. In 1861, Louisiana left the United States to become one of the **Confederate** States of America. The Northern states that remained in the United States said that the Southern states couldn't become their own country. The two sides fought the Civil War to decide whether America would be one country or two.

20

A PROTEST

AGAINST THE

ORDINANCE OF SECESSION,

Passed by the Louisiana Convention, on the 26th January, 1861, presented to the Convention on that day, by JAMES G. TALIAFERRO, the Delegate from the Parish of Catahoula, who asked that it might be entered upon the journal of the Convention, which was refused.

THE delegate from the parish of Catahoula opposes unqualifiedly the seperate secession of Louisiana from the federal Union, and asks leave to place upon the records of the convention his reasons for that opposition. They are as follow :

I oppose the act of secession because, in my deliberate judgment, the wrongs alleged as the cause of the movement might be redressed under the constitution by an energetic execution of the laws of the United States, and that, standing upon the guarantees of the constitution, in the Union, southern rights might be triumphantly maintained under the protection and safeguards which the constitution affords.

Because, in secession I see no remedy for the actual and present evils complained of, and because the *prospective* evils depicted so gloomily may never come ; and if they should, the inalienable right to resist tyranny and oppression might then be exercised as well and as successfully as now.

Because I see no certainty that the seceding states will ever be confederated again ; none that the border states will secede at all ; and if they should, I see no reliable ground for believing that they would incorporate themselves with the gulf or cotton states in a new government. I see no surety either that Texas would unite with them.

Because the gulf or cotton states alone, were they to unite in a separate confederacy, would be without the elements of power, indispensable in the formation of a government to take a respectable rank among the nations of the earth.

Because I believe that peaceable secession is a right unknown to the constitution of the United States ; that it is a most dangerous and mischievous principle in the structure of any government, and when carried into the formation of the contemplated confederacy of the gulf states, will render it powerless for good, and complete its incapacity to afford to the people permanent security for their lives, liberties and property.

Because it is my solemn and deliberate conviction that the distraction of the southern states by separate secession will defeat the purpose it is intended to accomplish, and that its certain results will be to impair instead of strengthen the security of southern institutions.

Because the proper status of Louisiana is with the border states, with which nature has connected her by the majestic river which flows through her limits ; and because an alliance in a weak government with the gulf states east of her, is unnatural and antagonistic to her obvious interests and destiny.

Because by separate secession the state relinquishes all its rights within the government; it surrenders its equal rights to the common territories, to the vast public domain of the United States and the public property of every kind belonging to the nation. And for this reason I oppose secession as being emphatically submission.

Because, secession may bring anarchy and war, as it will assuredly bring ruinous exactions upon property in the form of direct taxation, a withering blight upon the prosperity of the state, and a fatal prostration of all its great interests.

Because, the act of dissolving the ties which connect Louisiana with the federal Union is a revolutionary act that this convention is, of itself, without legitmate power to perform. Convened without authority of the people of the state, and refusing to submit its action to them for their sanction in the grave and vital act of changing their government, this convention violates the great fundamental principle of American government, that the will of the people is supreme.

JAMES G. TALIAFERRO,
DELEGATE FROM THE PARISH OF CATAHOULA

A document that shows Louisiana's formal declaration to leave the United States

Sherman on horseback during the Civil War

Back to the Army

~

William Sherman loved his job at the college. But when Lousiana left the United States in 1861, he knew what he had to do. He quit his job and left Louisiana because he loved the United States. He and Ellen returned with their family to Lancaster, Ohio, where they'd lived as children. After a month, they moved again, back to St. Louis, where Sherman became president of a railroad.

When the Civil War began, the army asked Sherman to return to lead troops.

Bull Run

~

Sherman's first major battle in the Civil War was the First Battle of Bull Run. This was fought in July of 1861. William and his soldiers lost the battle to the soldiers of the South. But William's men fought hard for him, and he showed that he had what it took to be a strong leader. After the war, his rank was raised from colonel to brigadier general.

Manassas: Bull Run was the name of a creek outside the town of Manassas. Sometimes the battles of Bull Run are called the battles of Manassas.

The Battle of Bull Run

24

A photograph that shows Union forces at Bull Run in 1861

March to Victory

~

Through 1862 and 1863, Sherman became one of the leading officers under General Ulysses S. Grant, the head of the Union army. He helped Grant win major victories in Mississippi and Tennessee.

A scene from the Battle of Chattanooga that took place in Tennessee in 1863

Abraham Lincoln: He was one of the greatest presidents of the United States. He was against slavery. By winning the Civil War, Lincoln kept the United States one country.

26

From left to right: Abraham Lincoln, Sherman (standing),
Philip Sheridan, and Ulysses S. Grant

In 1864, Sherman led thousands of troops on a march
through Georgia. They burned part of the city of Atlanta
and destroyed property. They thought this would make
the South give up. Then they continued to march to the
sea. They arrived at Savannah, Georgia, a few days
before Christmas.

Sherman sent a message to President Abraham
Lincoln saying, "I beg to present you, as a Christmas gift,
the city of Savannah." Early the next year, the
South surrendered.

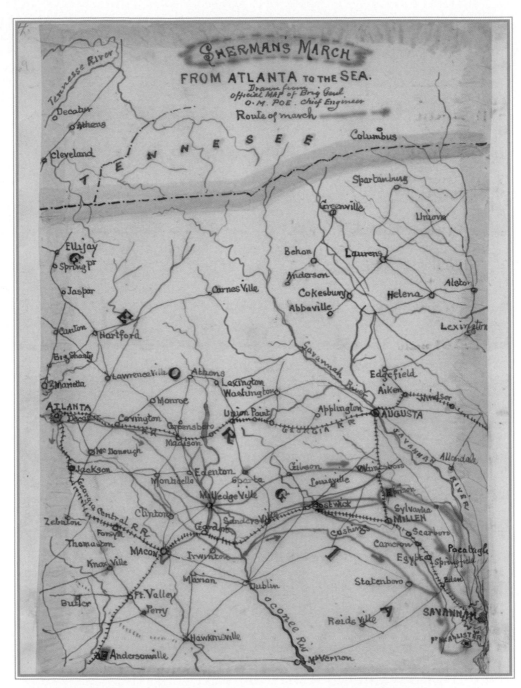

A map of Sherman's march to the sea in 1864

A War Hero

~

Sherman's march to the sea hurt the South, but it helped end the war. After the Civil War was over, Ulysses S. Grant was elected president. He then made Sherman the head of the U.S. Army in 1869. Sherman stayed in the army until 1884. He died on February 14, 1891, six days after his 71st birthday.

A photograph of Sherman taken shortly before he retired from the army

Important Dates to Remember

1820 Tecumseh Sherman is born.

1829 His father dies and "Cump" Sherman moves into the Ewings' house.

1836 Sherman enters the U.S. Military Academy.

1840 Sherman graduates from West Point. The army sends him to Florida.

1846 Sherman goes to California to fight the Mexican War.

1850 He marries Ellen Ewing.

1853 Sherman leaves the army and goes to work in a bank.

1857 Sherman becomes a lawyer.

1859 The Sherman family moves to Louisiana, where William becomes head of a new college.

1861 Sherman rejoins the army at the start of the Civil War.

1864 Sherman's troops march through Georgia and "to the sea."

1869 Sherman becomes leader of the U.S. army.

1891 William Tecumseh Sherman dies.

Glossary

Confederate (kon FED ur et) — a person, state, or soldier on the Southern side in the Civil War

frontier (frun TEER) — a land where not many people live, the wilderness

generals (JEN ur ulz) — the highest rank in the military

military (MILL ih TARE ee) — the armed forces

Seminoles (SEHM ih nolz) — a Native American tribe

slaves (SLAYVZ) — people who are owned by another person or persons

soldiers (SOHL jerz) — those who serve in the military

Tecumseh (teh KUM seh) — a famous Native American chief

troops (TRUUPS) — soldiers

Union (YOON yun) — the Northern side in the Civil War

Index

Further Reading

Kent, Zachary. *William Tecumseh Sherman: Union General* (Historical American Biographies), Enslow Publishers, 2002.

King, David C. *William T. Sherman,* Blackbirch Press, 2002.

Remstein, Henna R. *William Sherman* (Famous Figures of the Civil War Era), Chelsea House, 2001.

Websites To Visit

http://en.wikipedia.org/wiki/William_Tecumseh_Sherman
http://www.swcivilwar.com/sherman.html
http://encarta.msn.com/encnet/refpages/RefArticle.aspx?refid=761572785

About The Author

Don McLeese is an associate professor of journalism at the University of Iowa. He has won many awards for his journalism, and his work has appeared in numerous newspapers and magazines. He has frequently contributed to the World Book Encyclopedia and has written many books for young readers. He lives with his wife and two daughters in West Des Moines, Iowa.